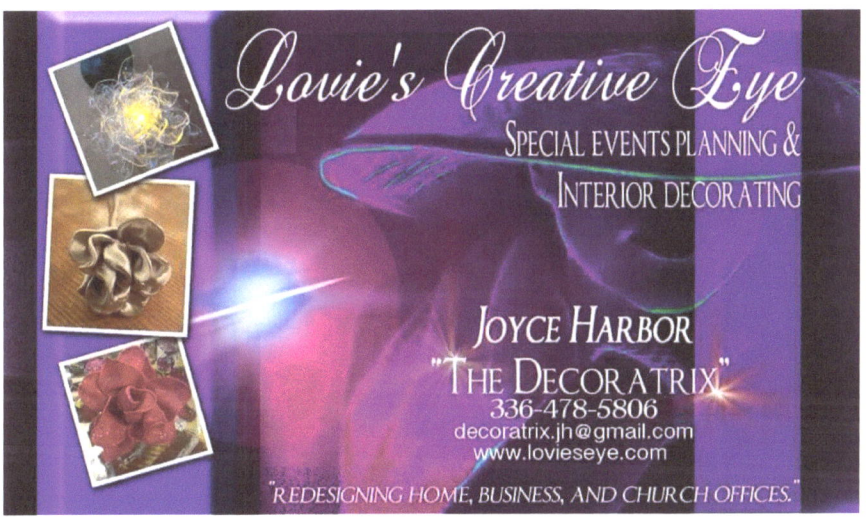

Lovie's

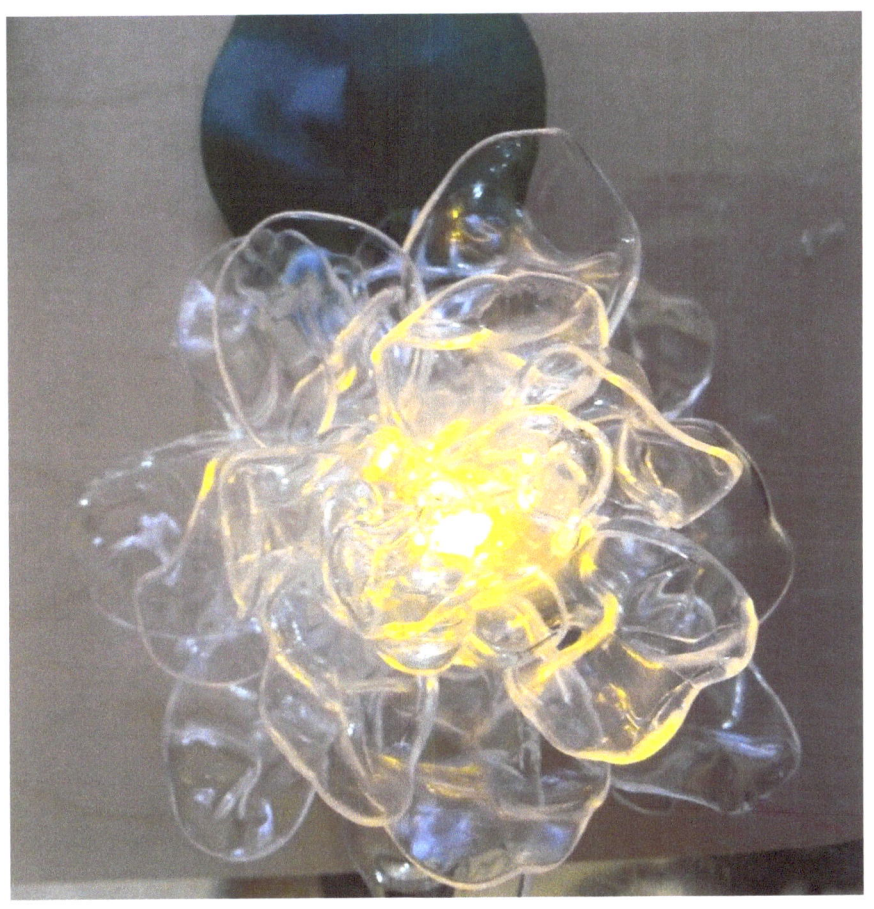

Professional Catalog 2015

Spoonies

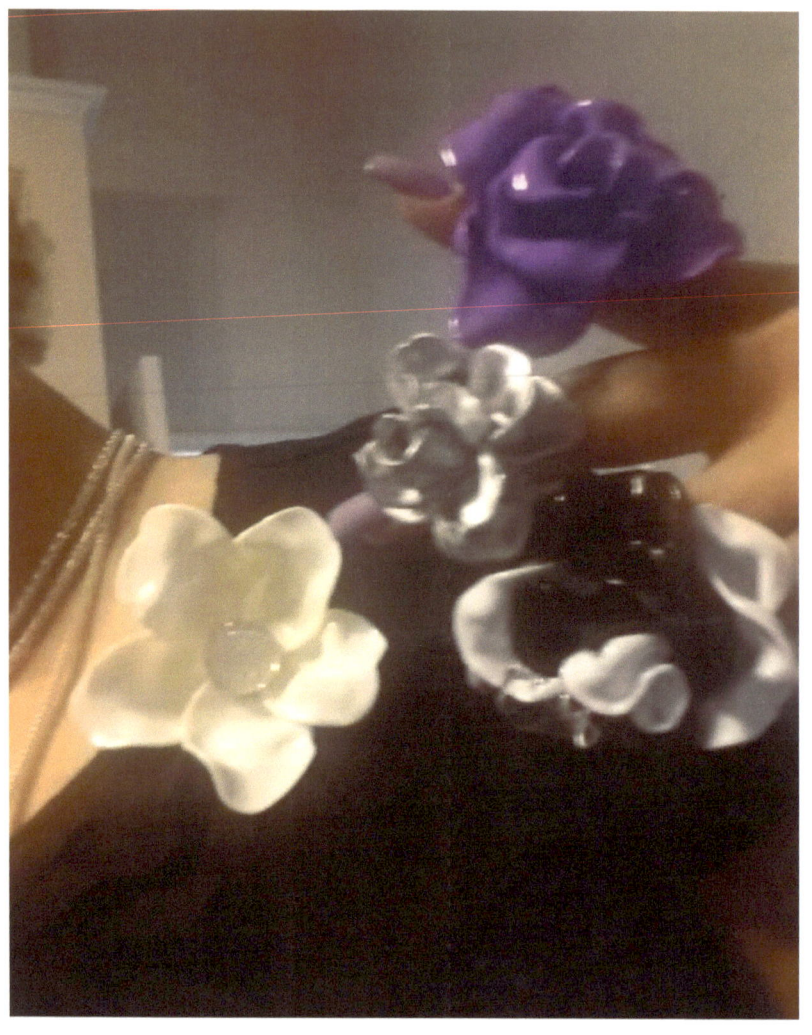

Sizes

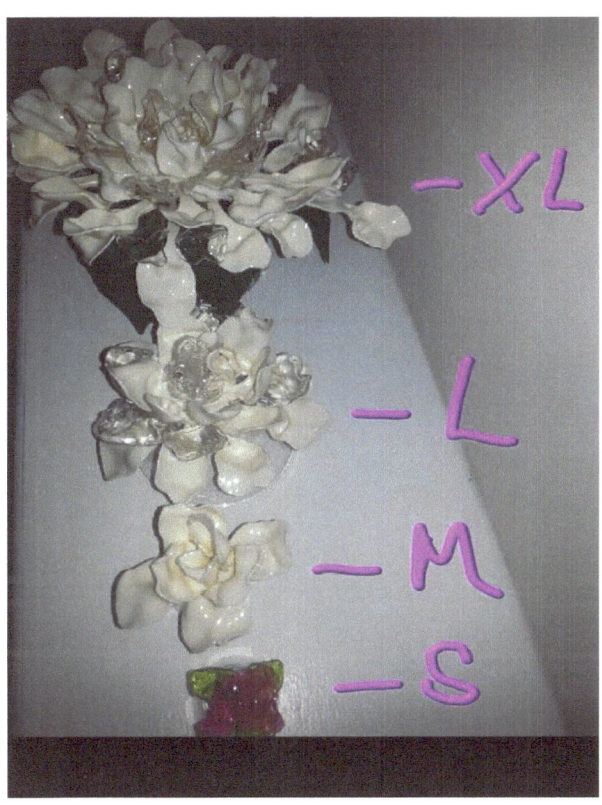

This is a general size price for the stand alone spoonies. Lights and other component change the price.

Small $6

Medium $10

Large $15

Extra Large $20

These fabulous broaches are $10! They are exquisite for accents for any wardrobe!

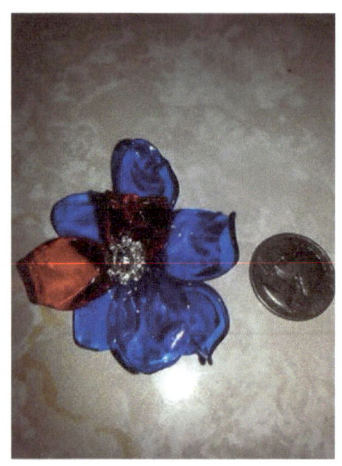
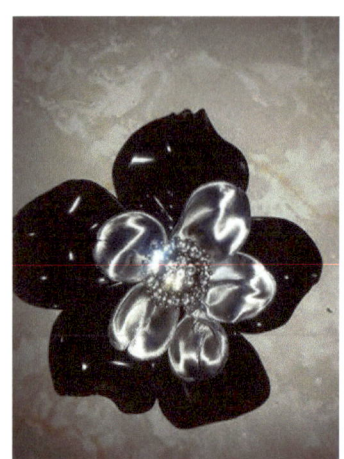

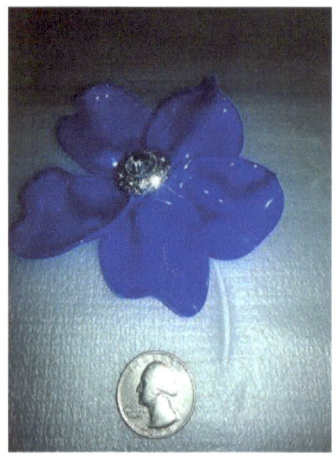

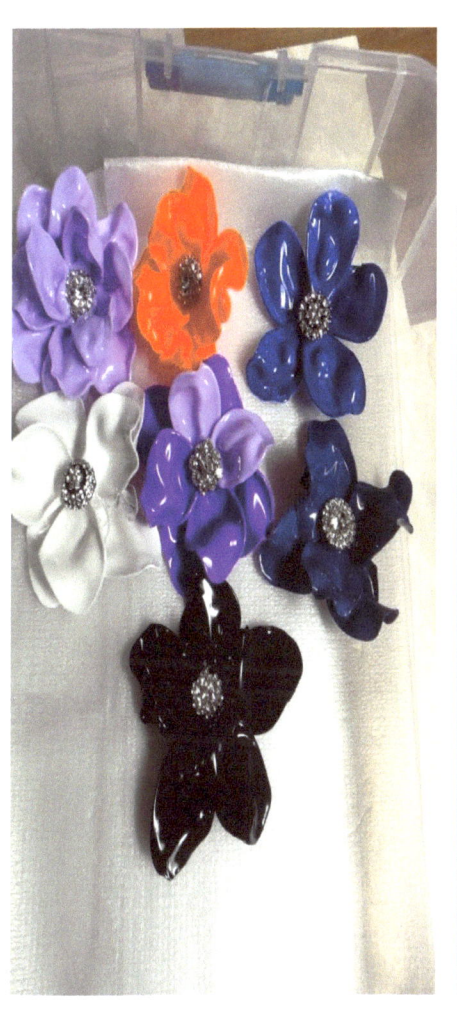
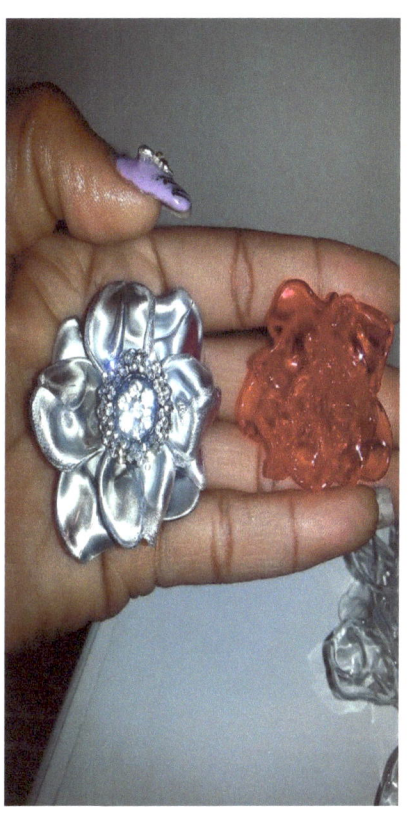

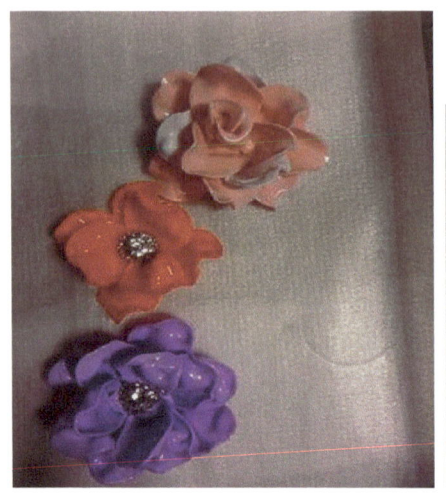

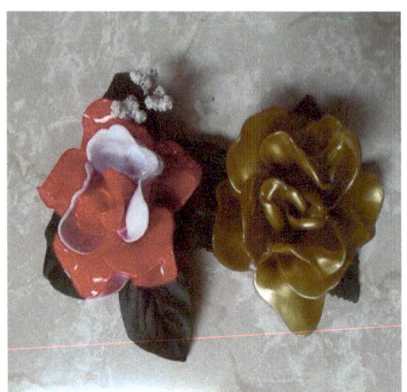

Mother's Day Broaches!

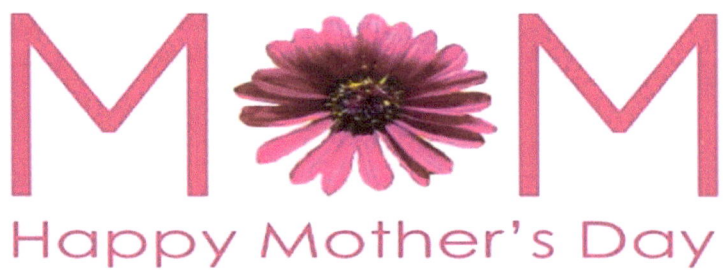

Happy Mother's Day

Sculptures and Centerpieces

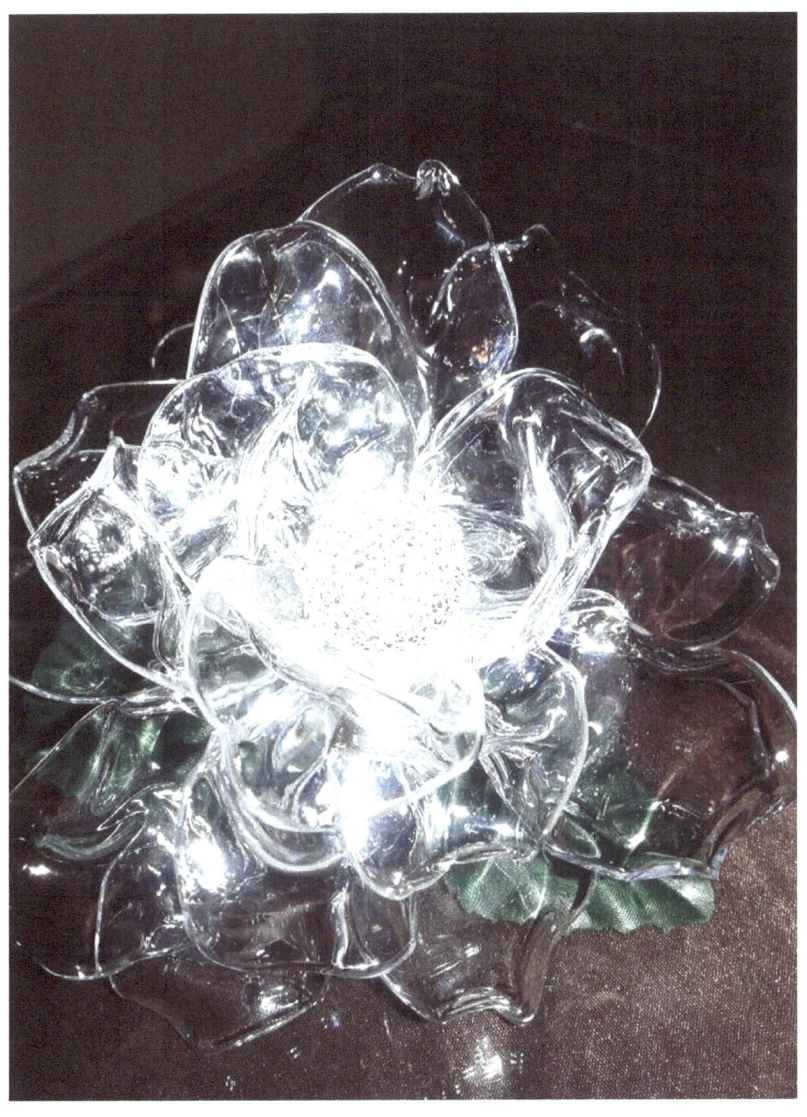

Stunning Scuptures add centerpieces add life to any room or table! Contact for specific prices!

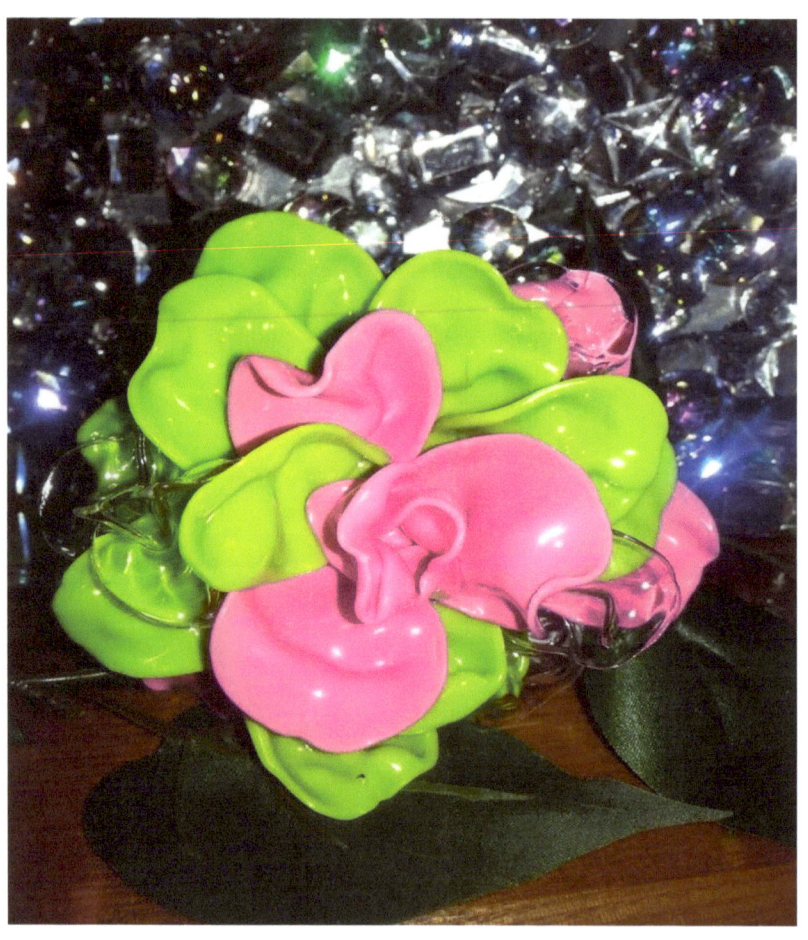

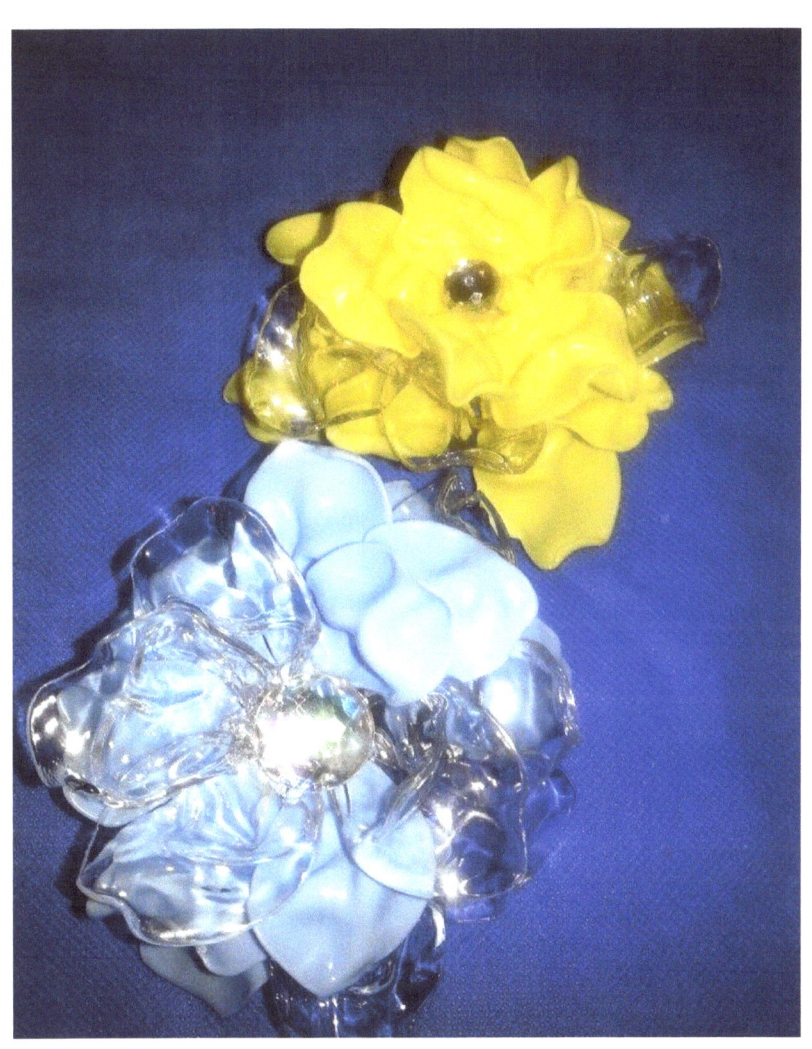

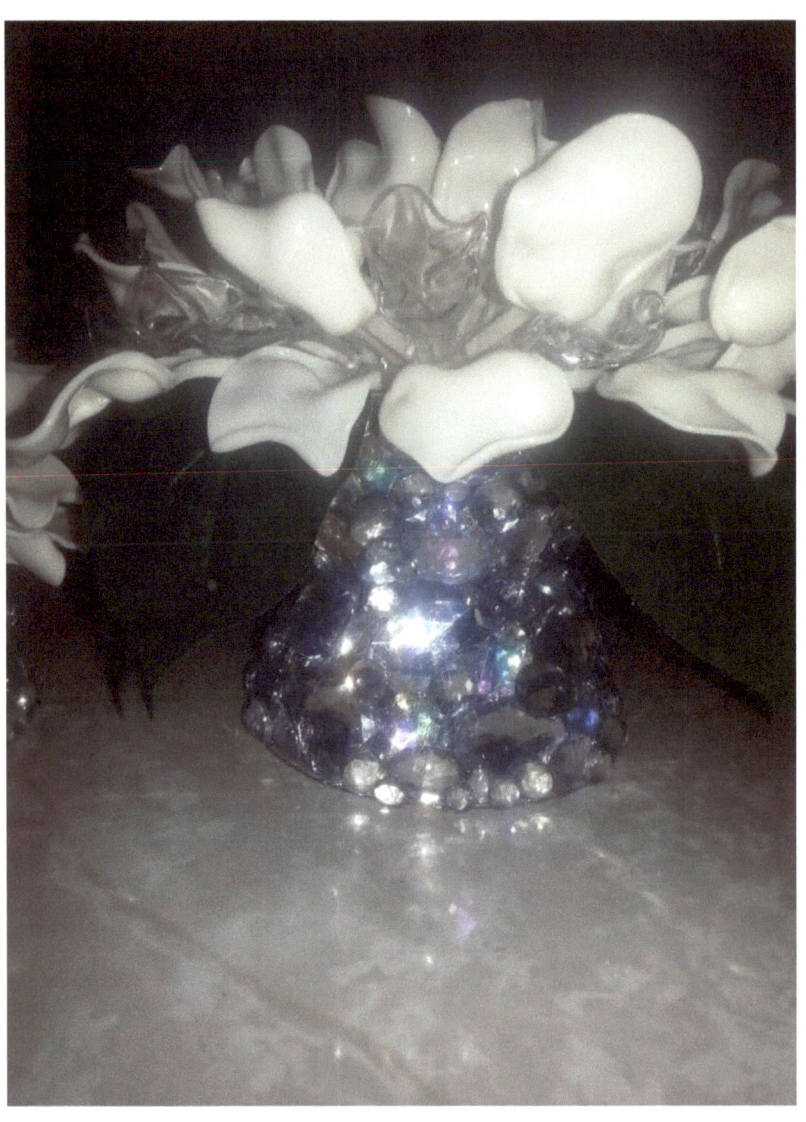

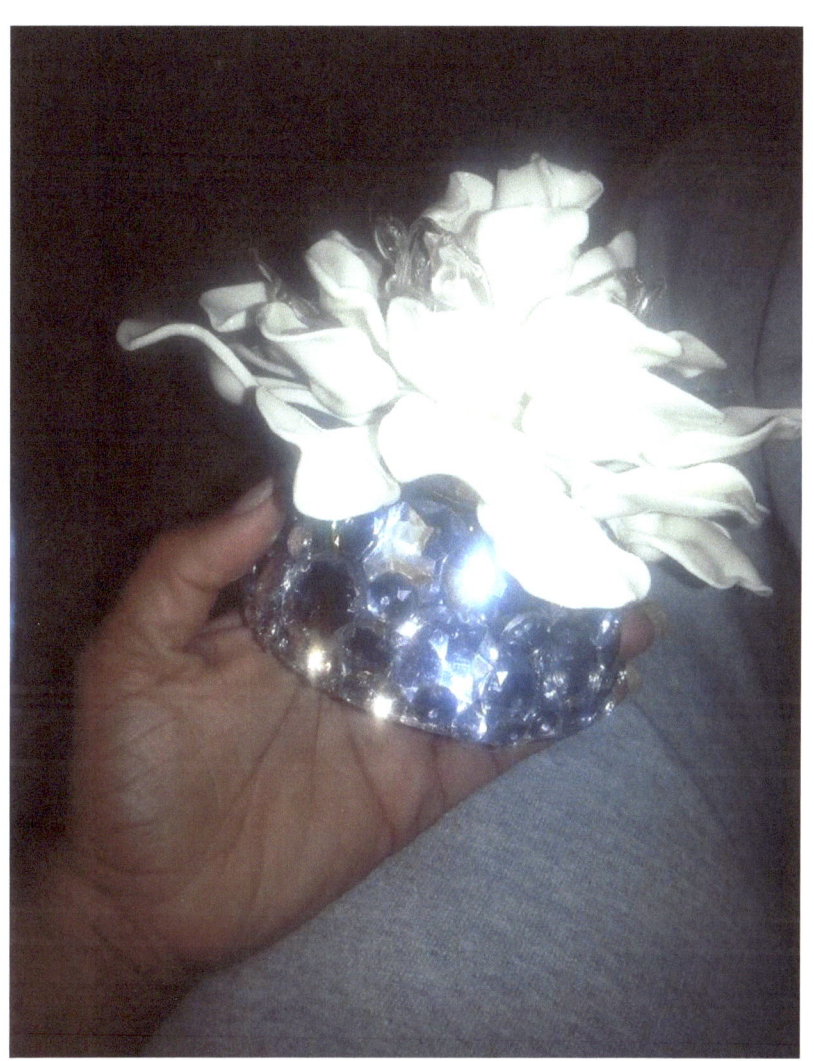

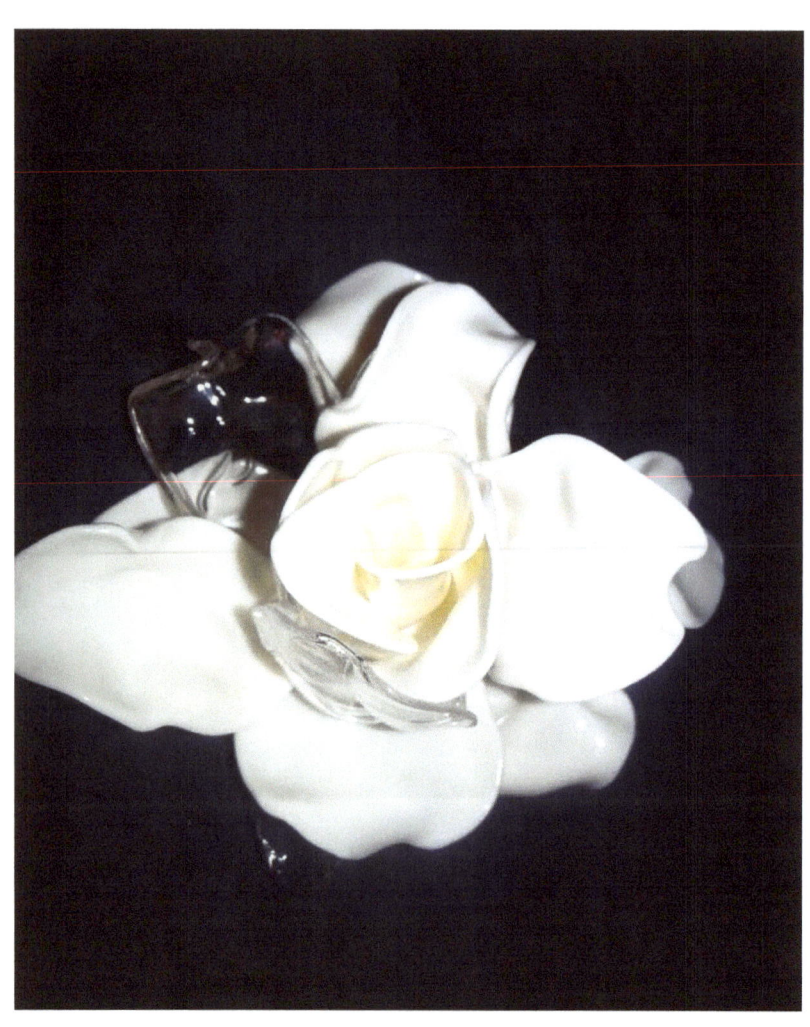

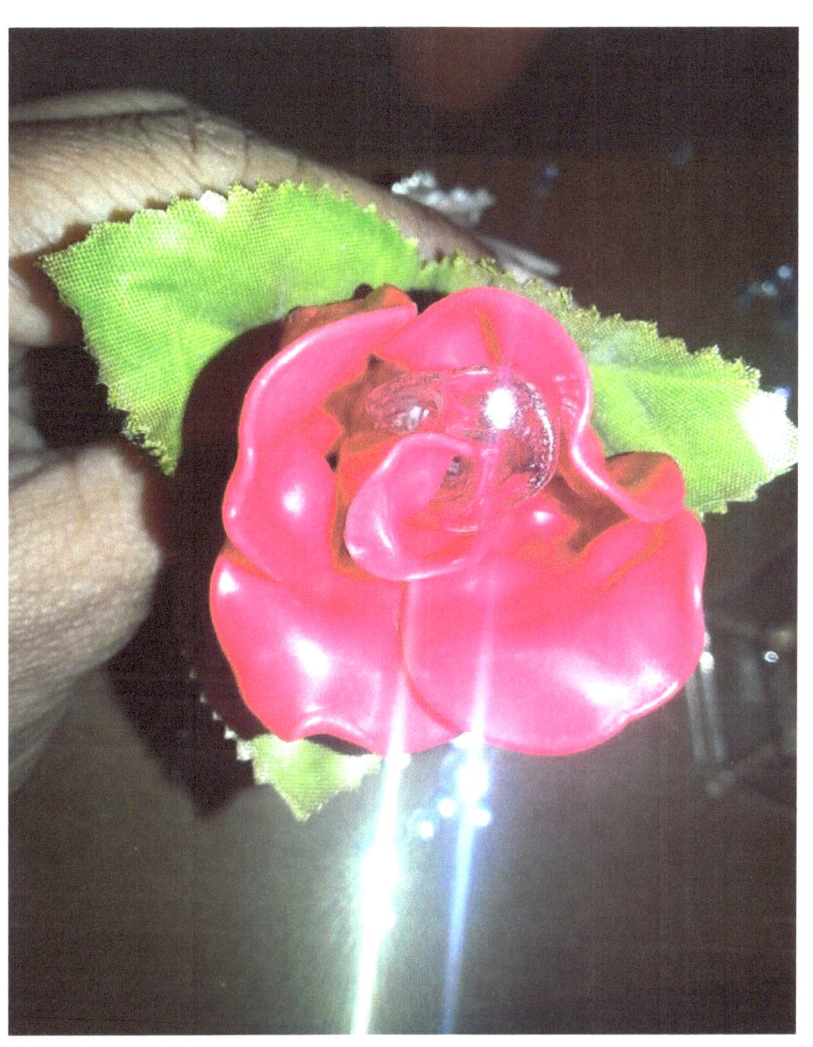

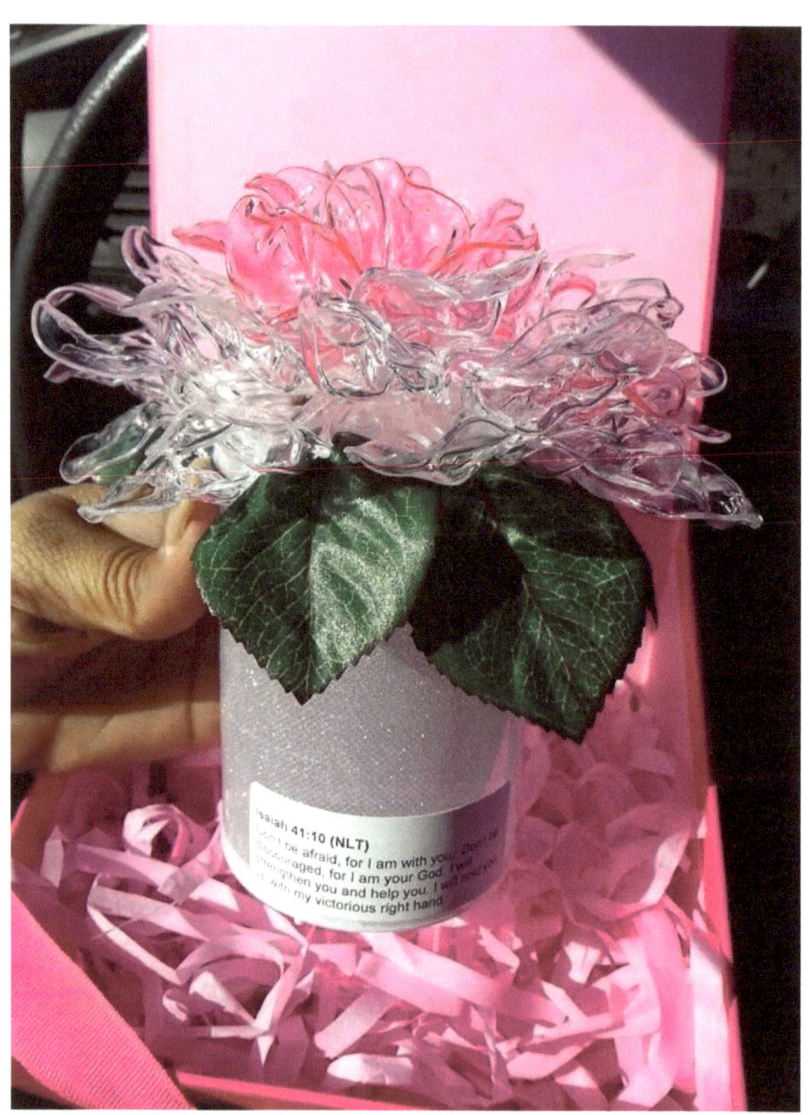

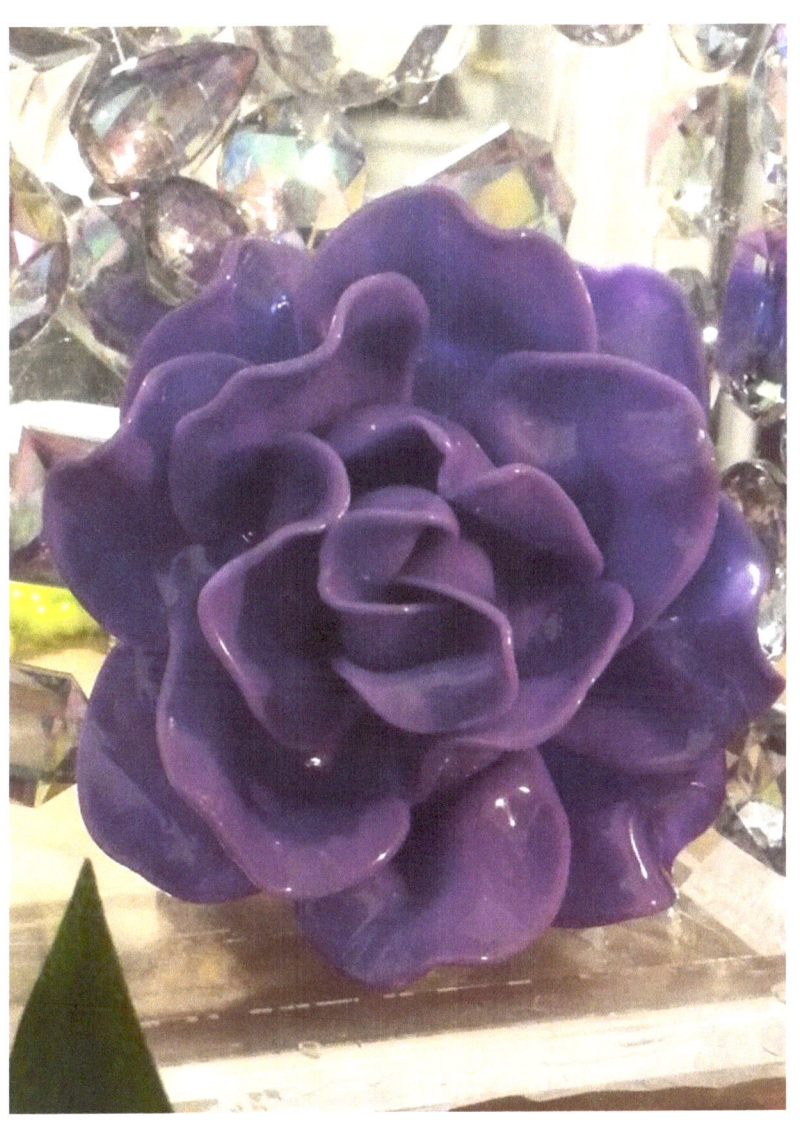

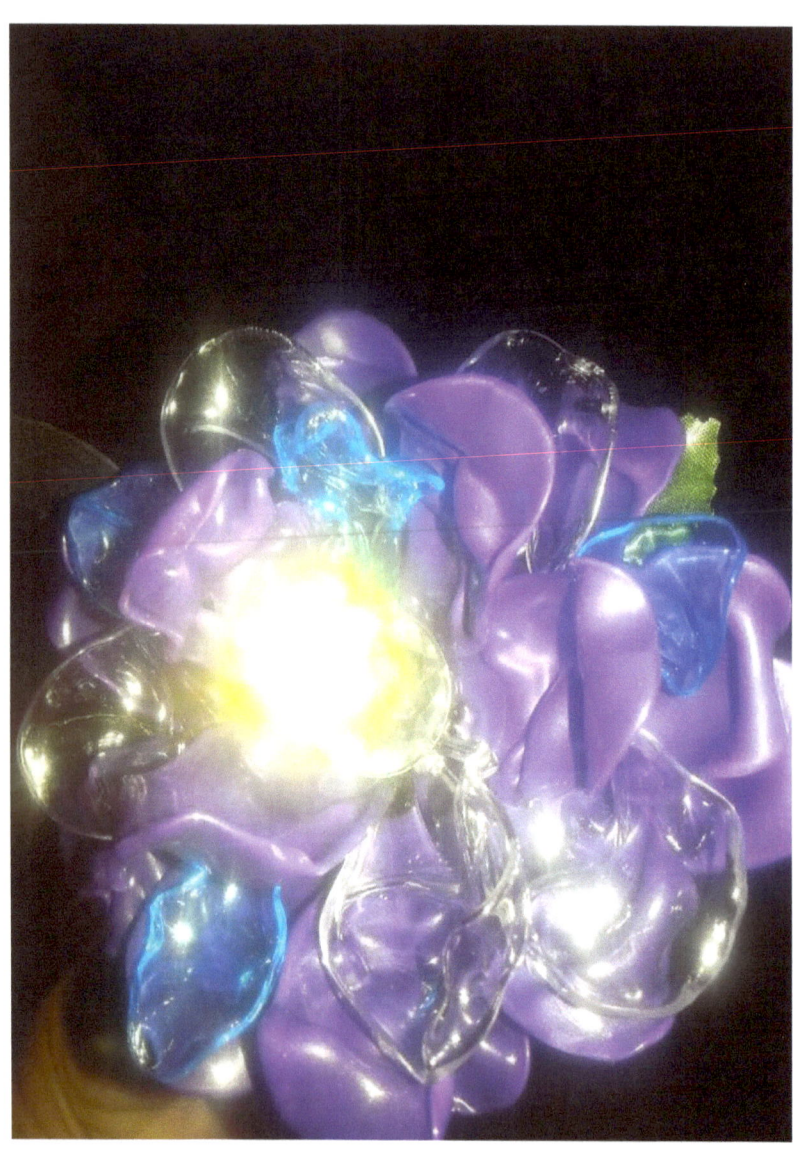

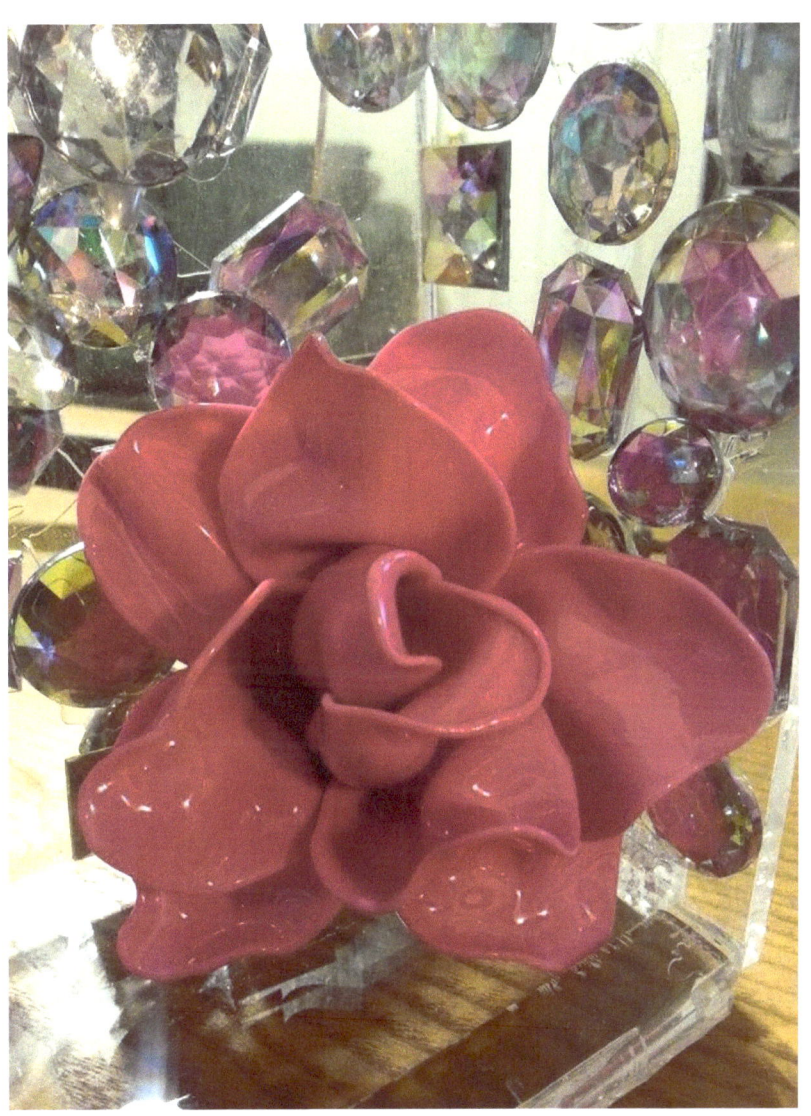

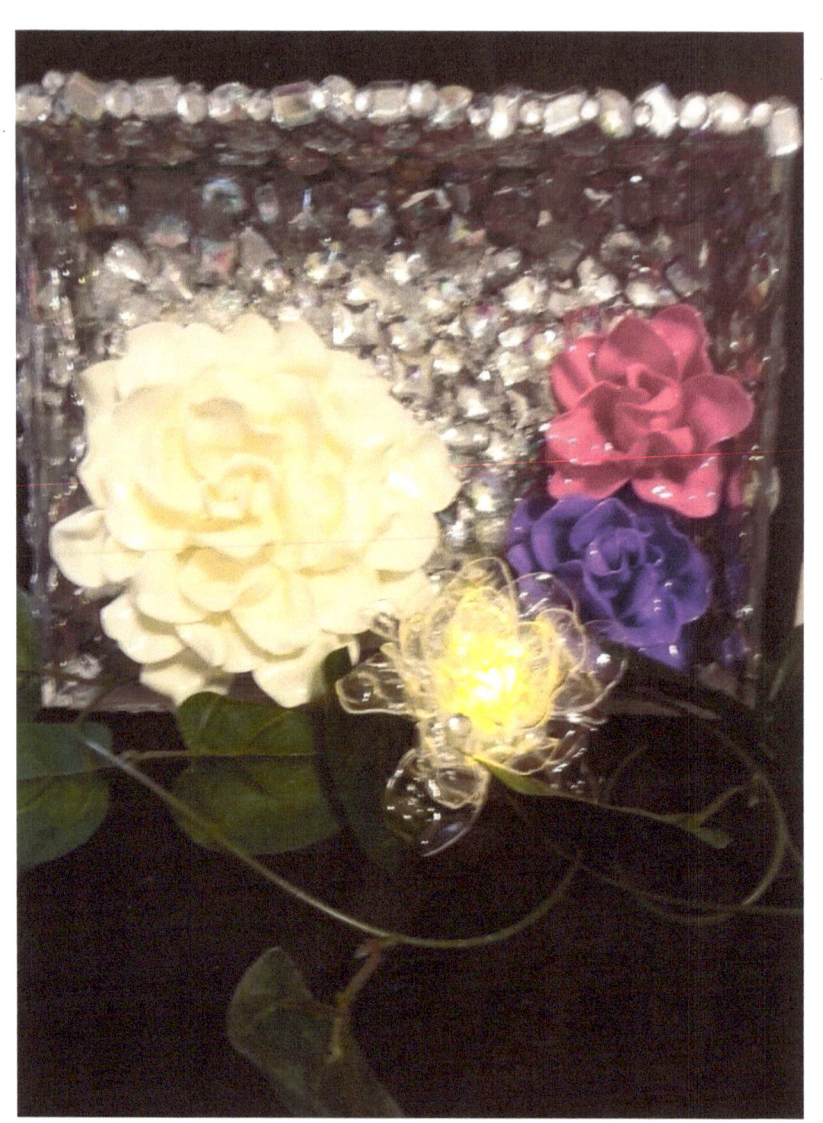

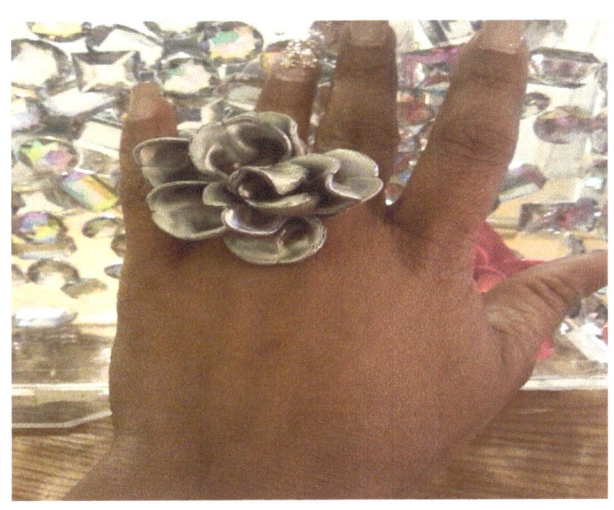

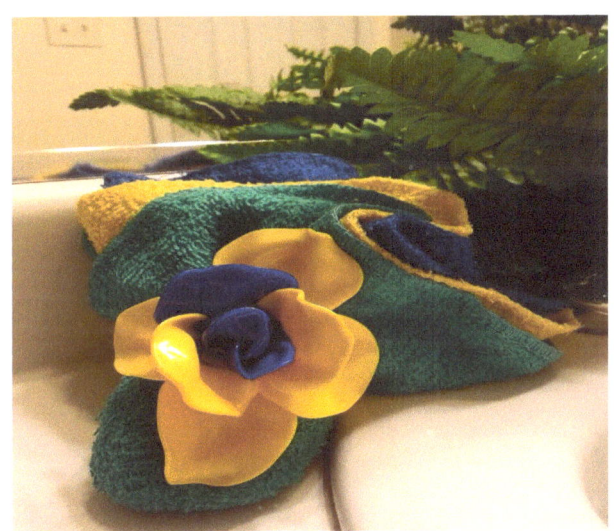

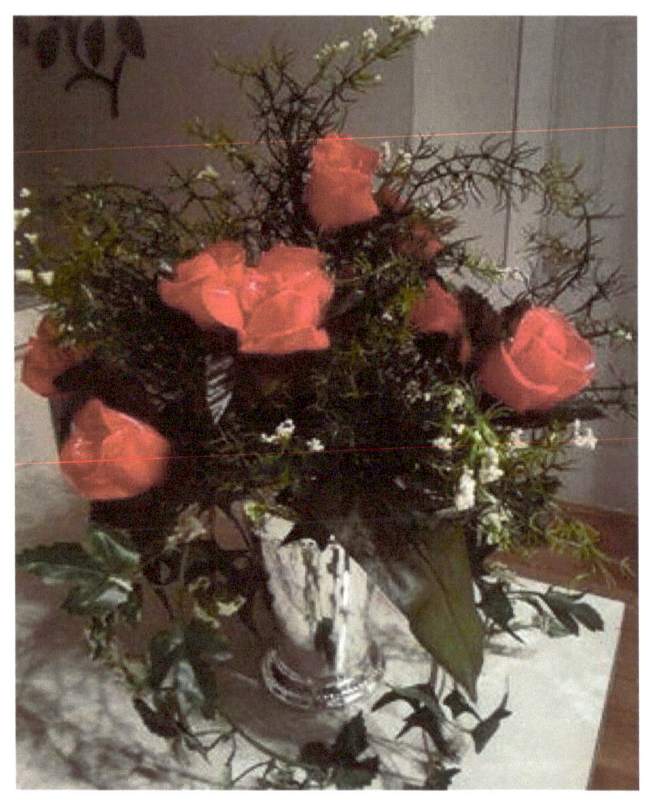

Our exquisite arrangements are perfect for all celebrations and special occasions! Contact us for specific prices!

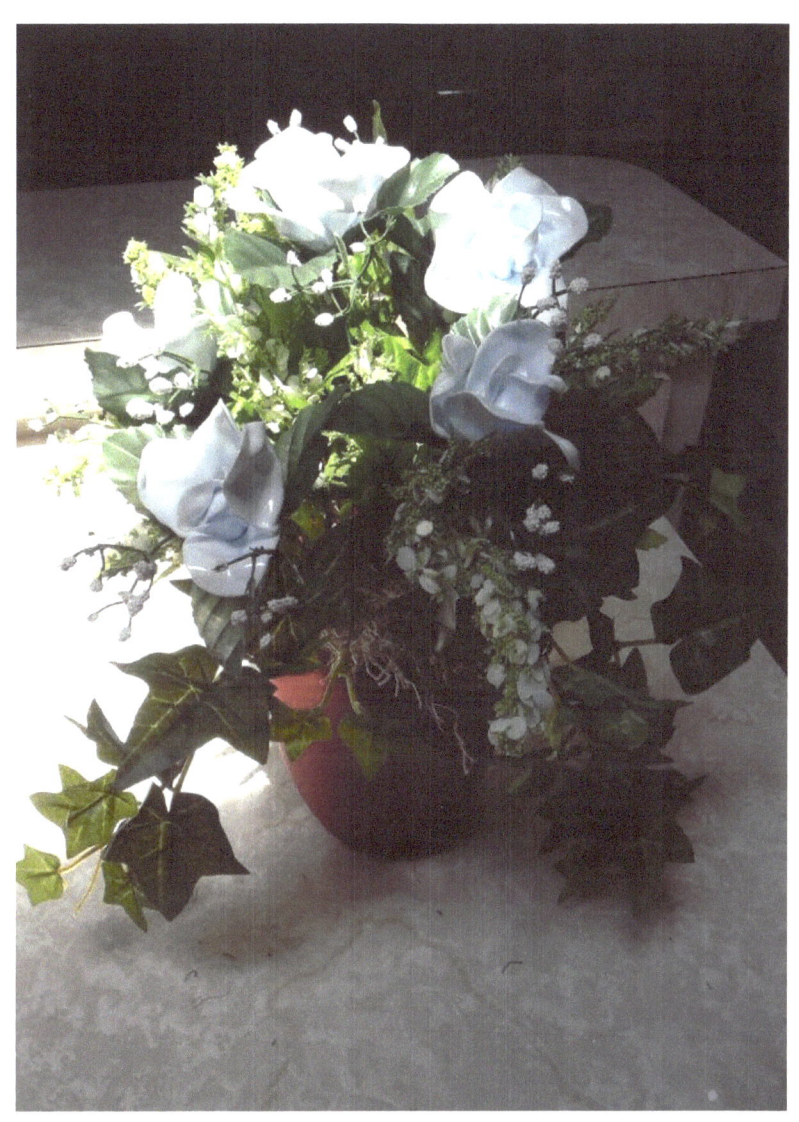

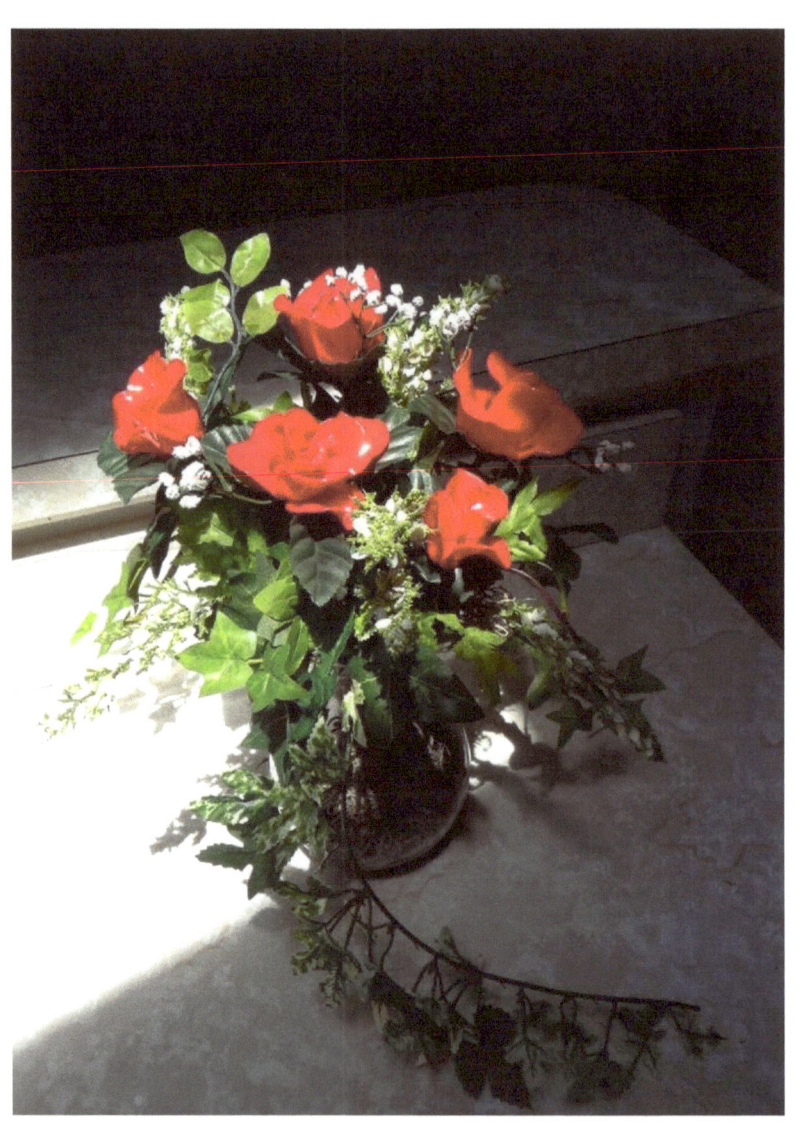

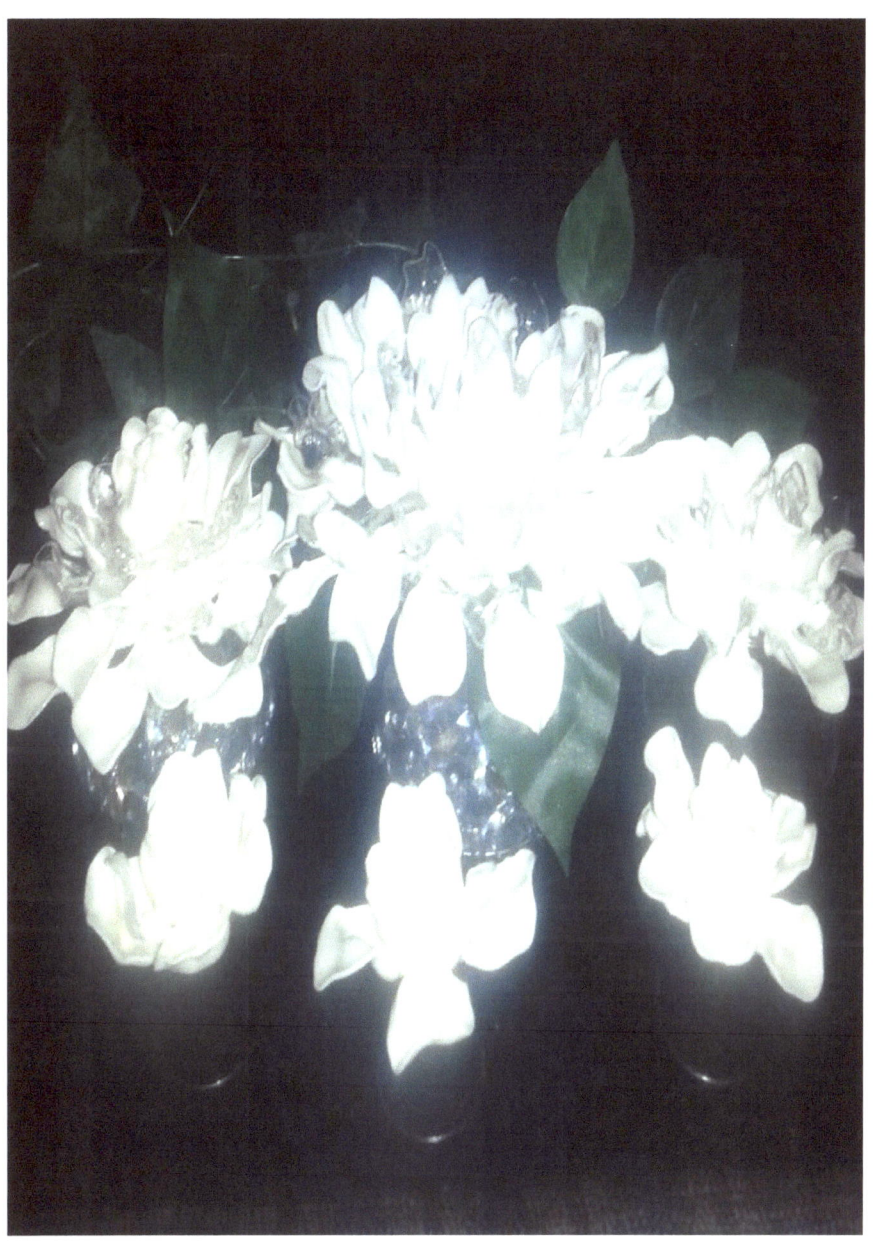

Personal Delivery!

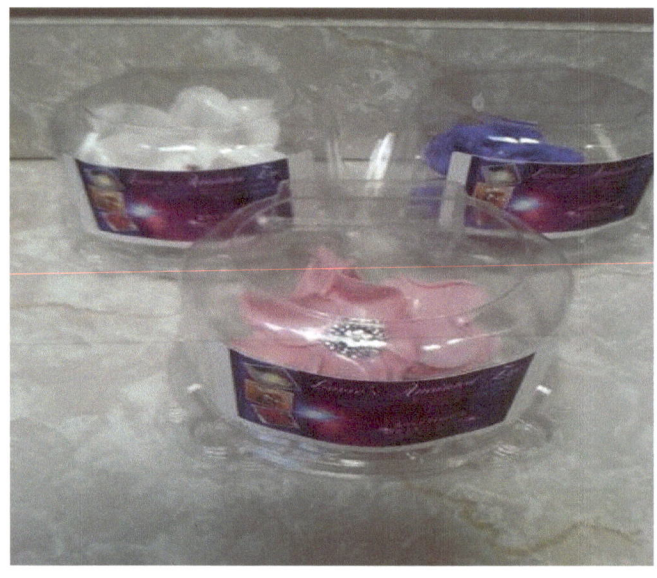

Here at, Lovie's Creative Eye, we have personal friendly delivery service! Make an appointment via telephone, email or Facebook!

New Direction Publishing

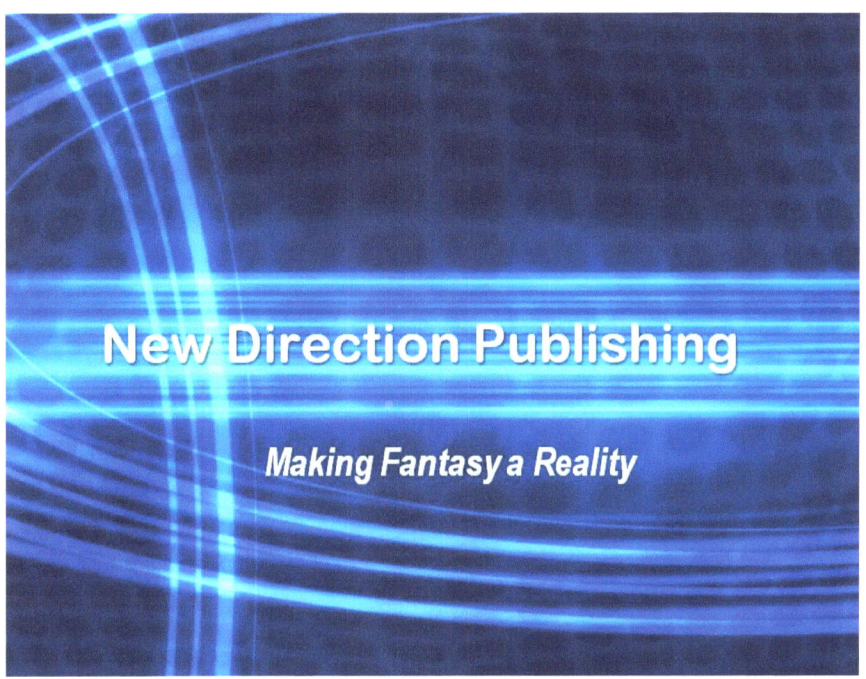

Phone: (336) 257-8459

Email: newdirectionpub@gmail.com

Website: www.facebook.com/newdirectionpub

Coming Soon!

From, *The Easy NDP Guide*:

The Three Steps

First, we explain our business.

Second, we ensure the client that the finishing product or outcome

will be published and released to the public as soon as it gets

reviewed.

Third the work is published.

After these three steps, that is when it is ready to be released. But,

before it is completed, we must abide by how the client wants their work

written, and typed. Successful clients want you to express their own

personal styles and make their dreams and fantasies come true.

The On-Demand Publishing Process

We publish through an on-demand publishing process. The on-demand process is used to help us spread people's ministries and canons, and their efforts are formed from their own individuality and ideas. This process is very different from the greedy and impersonal process that many large publishers undertake. A project should not take the average artist half or their personal savings. We do not believe or condone this type of oppression.

The Client Search: A Refreshing Journey

It is a journey to go around searching and attaining clients to help expand our business not for ourselves, but to liberate many people. We desire to help all ages, and ethnicities. We also desire to help all genders as well. People are being robbed everyday of all or most of their works. That is why we always legally copyright materials. This includes our company materials. This business is very difficult to manage, but it is can also be easy to gain real people that just want to help others, and be specific role models. This is a rapidly expansive contractual business!

www.ingramcontent.com/pod-product-compliance
Lightning Source LLC
Chambersburg PA
CBHW041614180526
45159CB00002BC/853